BRITTANY DE

FORGET YOU NOT

A guided grief & keepsake journal
for navigating life through loss

Hope

hope

Hope

CONTENTS

INTRODUCTION

Even though I'm so glad you're here, I wish we didn't have to meet this way. Your loss is, was, and will always be with you. And I'll never pretend to know the weight of your grief's impossible load, even as I carry my own. We're simply walking beside each other so that we feel less alone.

What we do share is a knowing. A depth of feeling that only losing someone you love exposes. A deep desire to understand and remember and commemorate our people in a forever kind of way. I'm heartbroken that you're here and also truly honored to help you use your own words to do just that.

In the act of writing and reflecting through these creative prompts, I hope you begin to feel some semblance of relief. Whenever you open this journal, I hope it feels like a safe place. A single source for all of your best memories to go into safekeeping. An heirloom to honor your loved one's legacy, and a place to freely share what can feel too vulnerable to outwardly express. I hope this journal helps you accept your pain, your love, and your longing and see how much these feelings change each time you sit down to write.

Because if there's one universal truth, it's that however you're experiencing grief right now, it won't be the place you stay.

MY STORY

I'm an artist: a watercolor painter and calligrapher. A writer. A loving mom and wife and sister and friend and daughter who still deeply misses her dad. I always will.

When I was thirteen years old, I heard the wheels of my mom's computer chair hurrying across the hardwood floor upstairs. Seconds later, her feet were missing stairs to get down to us.

I remember staring at her in unison with my sister, tears already streaming down her cheeks. "It's your dad," she managed to say as the three of us collapsed into each other. It was on that day, October 19, 2003, that my life changed forever. And it's been every day since that I've missed him.

When I was pregnant with our daughter in 2021, I found that becoming a mom after losing a parent stirred up more emotion than I was prepared for. Alongside the joy and excitement of bringing life into the world was the tragedy of my dad's death when I was just a child too. Some days I feel like he's right here with me, and on others I still can't catch my breath, even two decades later. It's a constant ebb and flow of comfort and pain, of growth and then retreat. A crushing reminder of time—both that it heals, and that grief seems to follow a path of its own.

"Am I going to be an eighty-year-old woman still crying about her dad?" I once asked my therapist, desperate through sobs.

"Yes. Yes, you will," she replied. "But it won't always feel this gut-wrenching."

I CREATED THIS JOURNAL BECAUSE GRIEVING
SHOULDN'T BE TABOO.

We've all experienced—or will experience—grief. I spent too many years beating myself up for perfectly normal feelings around losing my dad. What I wish I knew then is reflected here on these pages to hopefully be a comfort to you.

Pairing creativity with grief helped me cope with my dad's loss twenty years ago and these seemingly opposite forces continue to help me process and heal.

After he passed away suddenly, I journaled a lot. And I didn't know the long-term effect it would have on me to acknowledge and process what I felt during that time until much later in life, when I read and understood the research behind the journaling process.

You are a very special
Girl, The love within you
is felt by all those
around you. LOVE DADDY xoxxx

Writing helps us make sense of our catastrophic thoughts and experiences. The concentration it takes to form words and think carefully about each stroke puts us back into the present instead of being lost in thought. We don't need to have any answers or perfect sentences or beautiful prose. We just need to slow down and put pen to paper. And in the simple act of expressing ourselves, even if those words never see the light of day, writing lightens the load.

WRITING ALONE HAS A PROFOUND ABILITY TO HELP US HEAL.

When I fell in love with calligraphy and started my own art business much later into adulthood, I discovered that it's a moving meditation. Painting and writing and calligraphy aren't reserved for the artistically inclined. Creativity is inherent in all of us, and it's especially useful as a tool for expressing what would otherwise manifest as tornadoes inside our minds.

Please know, I wouldn't have been able to write this journal ten years ago. Maybe not even five years ago. It's only through time and acceptance of how chaotic and messy grief can be that I've learned to accept it as part of me, forever.

My future goal
is to be an artist.

Brittany

(WRITTEN AT AGE 10)

to
grieve
is to
love

I'm no longer weighed down every hour of the day. I'm living a full and joyful and truly happy life. But the sadness and despair still come, and those feelings are still at the center of every new experience. So, when the waves wash in, I've learned to sit with them. To write about it so that the space those thoughts occupy in my day and brain can be released to paper. To know that, as unfair as it often feels, this is normal. This is what it means to be in grief and to miss someone you love.

In many ways, I've come to learn, I grieved my dad long before he died. My dad suffered from alcoholism most of his life, but it doesn't define him. He loved us dearly, and he had his own internal battles. He died far too young, and he imparted more wisdom than he'll ever know. He created beautiful childhood memories for my sister and me, and he succumbed to his addictions.

I always loved him, and I always will. Two things can be true at once.

YOU CAN STILL LOVE AND FEEL HURT.
YOU CAN STILL GRIEVE AND FIND HAPPINESS.

Maybe you need those reminders too.

My dad's life and his death are the centerpieces of my life and have made me who I am. The pain of his loss changed me in ways I can only be grateful for. But the fact that I've grown because of my dad dying is a reality I wish I never had to face.

And so, this journal is how I'm honoring my dad, and how I hope to share a few steps in your journey too: steadfast in love, powerfully sentimental, shattered but wholly grateful for the privilege of living a wonderful life.

This is your journal to use as you need. Take what resonates and leave what doesn't. And know that the pages that hurt too much to touch right now will be there to return to when you're ready.

This journal isn't a replacement for therapy, and it's not a solution to grief. I wish it was, but there isn't one. There isn't a recipe for what to do when your world implodes. If there's one thing you absolutely must do, it's to remove the expectations you or others place on you for the time it takes to heal and how you should feel. Both are infinite. These pages are meant to help you put one foot in front of the other. To allow all your emotions to express themselves freely and not turn against yourself for feeling too much or for too long (there's no such thing). To understand your life through loss and navigate new paths while still carrying the load.

I've shared some of my own stories here to encourage you in yours, because it's through connection that we sometimes feel less alone. Let my words be merely a guide. A comfort. A jumping-off point when you're staring at a blank page or with a mind blanketed by the numbness or crushing reality of living in grief.

And, whenever possible, give yourself some time after writing here before going back to your regular day. Grief expert and author David Kessler suggests ending a writing session by telling yourself, "That was then, this is now," and recentering yourself back into the present. Acknowledge the room you're in. Activate all five of your senses. And always ask for a hug.

Chronos

Ordinary chronological time measured in hours, minutes, and days.
It's linear and sets a "limit" on our grieving.

Kairos

Felt time that's not subjected to the boundaries of chronos. It takes
as long as it takes. It's about integrating loss into your life and finding
purpose—not on a set timeline, but in the present moment.
This is the true experience of grieving.

WRITE TO

express

NOT TO

impress

KEEP COMING BACK

This is a journal that you'll want to come back to hundreds of times over the course of your life. Sometimes to reflect on passages you wrote months ago, and in others to respond to a prompt for the first time, which might have felt too raw when you last sat down to write.

I imagine that some pages will be for you and you alone, and others might be shared with friends and family when your memories become part of future moments. When writing, you might put into words for the first time what has been etched into your brain for years without realizing it. You might feel relieved to see it on paper, knowing that those stories and their wisdom are here now, whenever you need them most.

WHERE TO START

Just like life, loss isn't linear. And so, this journal doesn't have to be either. There's no end goal here. This isn't about "getting over," "moving on," or "forgetting" anything at all. You're simply moving forward. One step, one page, one word at a time.

REST

I encourage you to start with the Rest section every time you sit down to write, but there is no end.

Even after you fill in the last line of this journal, you can revisit those same questions years from now and notice how you'll write a completely different response. Similarly, flip through to see which quotes and artwork speak to your experience now, and how each new day or month will draw your attention elsewhere.

LETTERS TO YOUR LOVED ONE

There are blank pages in the back of this journal where you can write letters to your loved ones. Use these upon receiving this journal or whenever the feeling strikes. Write to your loved ones about your intention behind putting pen to paper. Expand on some of the creative prompts ahead. Tell them about a particularly hard or surprisingly good day when they made their love known to you. And remember: don't write to impress. We're simply here to express.

HOW DO I KNOW IF I'M READY TO WRITE?

Whether you received this journal as a gift, it came up in your search results, or it called to you from the shelves of your favorite bookstore, you have a big heart. You're sentimental and a bit nostalgic. Maybe you've never written before, but you want to honor who you lost, and you're afraid those memories might start slipping away. You want their legacy to be the roots of your life. And it will be.

Remember: you're not writing perfect prose. You're just putting pen to paper.

MY GRIEF IS FRESH

If you're holding this in your hands in the days after losing your loved one, I wish I could give you the air from my lungs instead. Grief is loud and all-consuming, and instead of commemorating you need only try to comprehend. Writing a single sentence, let alone a story about your last memory together, may feel far too exposed. I'm sure you hate hearing the phrases "Time heals," "I'm so sorry," and the well-meaning "How are you doing?", because these words don't remotely touch the depth of your despair.

Know that however you're feeling right now, it's valid and you're allowed to be "too" sad. Flip through to find quotes that resonate with you and spend time within the Rest, Cope, Reflect, Learn, and Letters to You sections until you feel comfortable surfacing legacy and memories. That time will come.

I'M NAVIGATING THE YEARS AFTER LOSS

Your sadness is just as valid on day one as it is decades later. Your joy is too. And if it feels impossible for the two to coexist right now, know that's okay, and know that they someday will. This journal is your companion: a place of safekeeping for all your memories with your loved one, and the ways their love continues through you for the rest of your life. I hope you find comfort here, especially in the Reflect section that starts on page 62.

I'M CONSIDERING MENTAL HEALTH SUPPORT OR THERAPY

I'm a huge advocate for therapy and waited way too long to attend my first counseling session. When I did finally go in my early thirties, it changed my life. Therapy is the reason I'm able to talk so freely about my experience and move past very specific blocks caused by my dad's traumatic death and the events leading up to it. Seeking mental health services is not a weakness—it's a strength. Read that again.

I'M IN CRISIS

Please know that you're loved, you're not alone, and help is available.

In the United States: To reach a trained crisis counselor for free, 24 hours a day, seven days a week, call or text 988. You can also go to 988lifeline.org or dial the current toll-free number 800-273-8255 [TALK].

In Canada: If you or someone you know is in immediate crisis, please call 1-833-456-4566 toll-free (in QC: 1-866-277-3553) 24/7 or visit talksuicide.ca. Text to 45645 (4 p.m. – midnight ET). You can also visit wellnesstogether.ca for more resources and to connect one-on-one with a counselor.

BetterHelp.com is an online counseling service currently available in the United States and Canada.

While you're writing, I hope your loved one's love for you makes itself known whenever you need it most.

And please know that . . .

Wherever you are in your journey, you're not alone.

Your loss was, is, and always will be with you.

You can't feel too much or for too long.

It's better to face your pain than avoid it.

It's worth navigating the new path ahead of you.

> HOWEVER YOU'RE EXPERIENCING GRIEF RIGHT NOW,
> IT WON'T BE THE PLACE YOU STAY.

Grief begins so loudly. Loss rings in your ears and your heart, reverberating across your entire body, your entire life. It's all-consuming and filled with sobs that leave you breathless because there is no air to breathe.

And as you begin to grow around it, with no rush and certainly no timeline, grief becomes quieter—a song coming on the radio, a video online, a card you found in storage with their handwriting, the smell of their laundry soap, holidays, and first milestones missed.

When joy and grief begin to coexist—and they will—it can feel jarring. The beauty of new views always exists in parallel to their loss. Forever part of the same formidable yet ever-changing landscape. The grief is always there but life still grows around it and how wonderful is that?

Rest

REST

What Is Mindfulness & How Can It Help Me?

....

Did you know that writing is a proven practice to help alleviate anxiety? Let's learn to get creative, not to be the best or to monetize your creations, but purely for all the tangible benefits: reducing stress, lowering your heart rate, activating your visual and motor skills, and even improving sleep. All things that we desperately need more of as we navigate the depths and chronicity of grieving.

In the earlier pages, I mentioned that art and writing inadvertently helped me cope with the loss of my dad two decades ago, and still do to this day. At the time, I didn't understand the research behind why. Beyond the benefits of processing emotions through words, I didn't realize that writing was a mindfulness practice and that it can be cultivated whenever you need it most.

WRITING IS RESTFUL—PHYSICALLY AND EMOTIONALLY.

And although it might seem counterintuitive, it can be a much better choice than mindless activities like TV and social media that numb us instead of creating space for our feelings. (Although, we all need to strike a balance.)

Especially in the early days of grieving, doing activities that make us feel safe and contained is a lifeline. By expressing yourself in this journal, you're less likely to be at a peak level of stress the next time another emotional storm comes. These tools will help you get back to a better baseline.

WRITING IS A

Moving Meditation

GRIEF IN THEORY:

DENIAL

GRIEF IN REALITY:

ANGER

BARGAINING

DEPRESSION

ACCEPTANCE

If the idea of sitting deep in thought right now sounds incredibly overwhelming, you're not alone. It's the reason I avoided traditional meditation for years (but now I see it as an incredibly helpful tool). Interestingly, writing puts you in the present even as you write about the past. Because of that, you get to experience the many benefits of mindfulness. Trust me—it's not as "woo-woo" as you might think.

When you write, you're not multitasking. Writing is a monotask that forces you to stay present. When you start paying attention to other small parts of the writing experience, like the sound of the pen on your paper, the way the ink flows across the page, and the concentration it takes to form each letter, you'll become even more absorbed in the moment. This intentional focus on one thing at a time, and the repetitive strokes, turns writing into a moving meditation.

Whether your grief is fresh or you're navigating life years after your loved one's loss (see pages 16–17 for more), the effects of mindfulness and meditation are well-researched and evidence based. This might be your first foray, or you might be well-versed already. Either way, practicing becoming more present can help you experience a whole-body calm when you desperately need it most.

ALWAYS START HERE

Every time you sit down to write, try starting here and giving yourself dedicated time and privacy. Do the exercises on page 30 and 31 to give yourself as much of a peace boost as possible. Some days will feel different than others. Give yourself the grace, patience, and openness to try it each day in a few different ways.

Part of being ready to write about such a difficult subject matter is not feeling like you're going to be judged or criticized. This journal is for you and you alone. You're not trying to impress anyone or write perfect prose.

The idea behind freewriting is to respond to a prompt quickly without stopping to reflect or rewrite it. You can also respond to these freewriting prompts on a sticky note if you want something less permanent. Write whatever immediately comes to mind without judgment or reflection. Try not to let your internal editor come out.

Based on your answers to the following statements, try to emulate that space for yourself. You might say that classical music brings you peace today, and you feel safest sharing your thoughts when you know no one else but you can read them. You might be comforted by looking through old photos one day or by the sound of your pet sleeping beside you the next. Answer quickly, honestly, and without judgment.

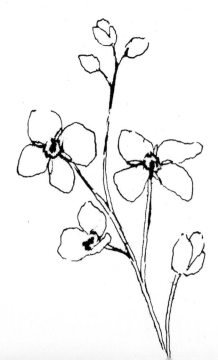

DATE: ....

Each time you sit down to write in this journal, ask yourself the same questions, freewrite your responses, and try to create a space for yourself that honors your answers.

MY GRIEF FEELS ....

....

....

....

A SONG OR SOUND THAT BRINGS ME PEACE IS ....

....

....

....

I FEEL SAFEST SHARING MY THOUGHTS WHEN ....

....

....

....

RIGHT NOW, THESE THINGS BRING ME COMFORT: ....

....

....

....

Each time you return to this section, respond to this prompt quickly without stopping to reflect or rewrite it. You'll soon see a wave of different reflections showing you the peaks and valleys of your experience.

Naming your emotions is proven to reduce their intensity. By leaning into how you feel, the frequency and intensity of those feelings will decrease over time. Denying how you feel has the opposite effect. In generations past, we believed that what we didn't talk about ceased to exist, but blocking how you feel actually does the most harm in the grieving process.

I'M FEELING . . .

(NUMB) (ANGRY) (GUILTY) (OVERWHELMED) (STRESSED) (ISOLATED)
(ANNOYED) (LONELY) (FRAGILE) (PRESSURED) (UNFOCUSED) (EMPTY)

WHAT GIVES ME HOPE?

The tools ahead will help train your mind to focus on the present instead of on spiraling thoughts. I would never try to minimize your pain or simplify the most complex human emotion (grief) into a few basic shapes—these exercises are simply proven to help train your awareness and give you a sense of stillness and clarity.

By starting here, you'll be able to answer the creative prompts on the pages ahead in a more stable state. Instead of being at a level ten of anxiety or stress at all times, you'll now have some tools to help bring you down and cope with more difficult days when you're not already at max capacity. The best part? The benefits of mindfulness (page 25) can be experienced immediately, and for the long term.

Every time you open this journal, try to spend ten to fifteen minutes learning and practicing the following mindfulness exercises that I teach in all my calligraphy workshops. Already filled the pages? Draw simple boxes in any notebook at home. You can do all of these exercises repetitively when you need your mind to rest. No special writing instruments are needed: experiment with a pen, pencil, or markers, and use any colors you like.

Focus on moving slowly, paying attention to the sound of the pen on the paper, the way the ink flows onto the page, and the concentration it takes to start and end each stroke intentionally.

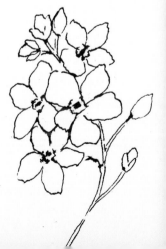

BREATHING EXERCISE 1

CIRCULAR THOUGHTS: Breathe in for seven seconds when you're moving in an upward motion. Breathe out for eleven seconds when you're moving in a downward motion.

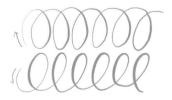

BREATHING EXERCISE 2

FIGURE-EIGHT KNOT: Starting on the left, trace the full length of the shape while inhaling, and then trace the full length again while exhaling. Continue this practice for five minutes, switching directions halfway through.

BREATHING EXERCISE 3

IT COMES IN WAVES: Draw the full length of your inhales and exhales so that the rate of your movement is the same as your breathing. Your breath might start shallow and rapid, and then the lines will get longer as more time passes and you feel more relaxed.

YOUR TURN

EXERCISE 1

EXERCISE 2

EXERCISE 3

SIMPLE DRAWING EXERCISE: PEBBLES

The only "rule" is to make sure at least one edge of your next pebble connects to the one you just drew. Once you've filled the page, color in the white space between each pebble.

EXAMPLE:

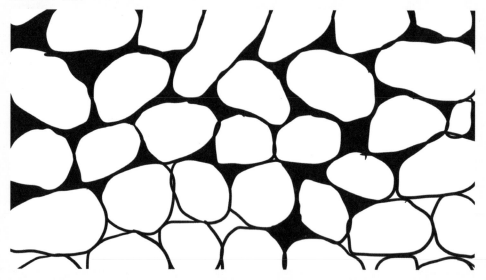

YOUR TURN:

MORE WAYS TO PRACTICE MINDFULNESS
THROUGH GRIEF

STEP I: ACTIVATE YOUR SENSES. When you're feeling particularly anxious, try activating all five of your senses. You can do this anywhere, anytime to regulate your emotions and feel grounded again.

TEN THINGS I SEE:

① _____

② _____

③ _____

④ _____

⑤ _____

⑥ _____

⑦ _____

⑧ _____

⑨ _____

⑩ _____

FIVE THINGS I CAN TOUCH:

① _____

② _____

③ _____

④ _____

⑤ _____

THREE THINGS I HEAR:

① ....

② ....

③ ....

TWO THINGS I SMELL:

① ....

② ....

WHAT I CAN TASTE:

....

....

....

Then breathe in for seven seconds and out for eleven seconds, three times.

BREATHE IN. . .

$$1 \rightarrow 2 \rightarrow 3 \rightarrow 4 \rightarrow 5 \rightarrow 6 \rightarrow 7$$

BREATHE OUT. . .

$$1 \rightarrow 2 \rightarrow 3 \rightarrow 4 \rightarrow 5 \rightarrow 6 \rightarrow 7 \rightarrow 8 \rightarrow 9 \rightarrow 10 \rightarrow 11$$

STEP 2 : SET UP A BASIC ROUTINE. You're already exhausted, emotionally and physically. Even seemingly small decisions like what to wear when you wake up in the morning can add to the overwhelm.

Adding some structure to your days will limit the endless stream of choices to make. When you wake up, can you spend fifteen minutes writing every morning? Can you go to bed at the same time most evenings and go for a daily walk?

Most people think of structure as a lack of freedom, but routine is freedom when the rest of your world feels out of control.

STEP 3 : GETTING OFF TRACK AND BACK ON AGAIN. Similar to the theme throughout this journal, how you're feeling now won't be the place you stay. If you spent days in bed and were unable to use any of these tools, that's okay. Really. You're getting through life the best you can right now.

TRY AGAIN. IT'S WORTH NAVIGATING
THE NEW PATH AHEAD OF YOU.

Although we wish we could, we won't remember every word our loved ones shared with us. Is there a quote your loved one often said, or song lyrics they always sang? What quotes have you read that remind you of them or of the experience of living their loss? Returning to these words of wisdom may comfort you on particularly heavy days. Keep adding them here whenever you come across words that speak to your experience, or when you remember a piece of treasured advice they shared that you never want to forget.

It will always pain me that I can't hear my dad's voice anymore or remember all the funny or quirky things he would say. But every so often I see a quote while scrolling online or in a book that reminds me of him, or of the experience of living through his loss, that feels like a warm hug.

Write your words of comfort and wisdom in the boxes on the right.

Cope

COPE

Living With Your Loss

....

As much as your life has changed, somehow the world keeps turning. You're putting one foot in front of the other, but the familiar walls of work feel like another planet. You're caring for children or existing in a home that now feels like a foreign place. You go to call them in the car and are struck by the realization that, yet again, you can't. You're living in a present devoid of your past and it's jarring. Some days feel particularly heavier than others.

Even after decades have passed, there will still be these moments or days or weeks when the wound gets exposed again. When you've lost your footing and you ask yourself, "How am I still so sad?"

BUT YOU'RE ALLOWED TO BE.

The key is to accept how you feel, release it (writing is a great way to feel safe in doing so), and start again with self-compassion throughout the process.

It can be helpful to be aware of your triggers and accept that they will appear throughout your journey. That doesn't mean you haven't grown. It's a normal part of the process that we need to accept instead of battle.

By using the mindfulness techniques in the Rest section of this journal (page 20) and being open and accepting of how you're feeling, these particularly heavy days can be just that: heavy and often all-consuming. That doesn't mean every other day will feel this way, but it's important to allow yourself the space to feel the big waves when they wash in, knowing that they'll inevitably wash away and be less intense the next time.

grief is a
wound
that
never fully
heals

GRIEVING THROUGH CELEBRATION

The days we're meant to celebrate, like birthdays, anniversaries, and firsts, often remind us of who we're grieving instead. When I was pregnant with our daughter, the immense joy and excitement of bringing life into the world was felt right alongside the tragedy of my dad's death, both existing in parallel. These big days and uncomfortable feelings are allowed.

THESE ARE THE DAYS THAT I HAVE MISSED OR WILL MISS YOU THE MOST (anniversaries, milestones, a special day in your relationship, etc.):

_____

_____

_____

_____

_____

_____

_____

_____

_____

ON THOSE DAYS I MISS YOU MOST, WHAT DO I NEED (support, alone time, a book, an item of yours to hold on to, etc.)? _____

_____

_____

_____

_____

_____

_____

_____

_____

_____

You need to feel to heal

IDEAS FOR COPING ON DIFFICULT DAYS

Remember: it's always better to face your pain than avoid it. Set aside some uninterrupted time to really feel what you need to. Even if you're at work or in public when heavy feelings set in, plan to set aside time later that day or in a few days to sit and acknowledge what happened. The next time those same feelings hit you, they won't be as intense or happen as frequently if you allow them to come out.

Here are some ideas. Choose the ones that sound comforting and come back to this later when you need it.

DID YOUR LOVED ONE HAVE A FAVORITE RECIPE?

Even though your rendition won't taste exactly the same, our senses (particularly smell) are powerful stimulants of memories.

DATE COMPLETED: ....

WRITE YOUR LOVED ONE A LETTER...

...on their birthday or a day you just listed. Use the Letters to You section in the back of this journal.

DATE COMPLETED: ....

TELL STORIES...

...with friends and family that make you laugh and cry.

DATE COMPLETED: ....

FREE WRITE...

...about a thought, fear, or idea that you're stuck or ruminating on. Releasing it will reduce its power over you, both in the moment and in the future.

DATE COMPLETED: ....

TAKE A WALK OUTSIDE.

It's simple but proven to help clear a cluttered mind, especially when you're surrounded by nature.

DATE COMPLETED: ....

SURROUND YOURSELF...

...with loved ones who will listen. Ask for hugs freely.

DATE COMPLETED: ....

GIVE BACK TO YOUR COMMUNITY.

Support a cause that's important to you. Offer an extended hand to a neighbor. Even if it seems counterintuitive, helping others is proven to help our own well-being. It fills our cup instead of draining it even further.

DATE COMPLETED: ....

GO BACK TO THE EXERCISES...

...in the Rest section to regain some stillness and presence before going back to your regular routine. The breathing exercises are particularly helpful in a triggering period of time.

DATE COMPLETED: ....

LISTEN TO THE PLAYLIST...

...you created in the Reflect section that reminds you of your loved one.

DATE COMPLETED: ....

GO THROUGH PHOTOS OR MEMENTOS...

...slowly and intentionally. Then put them away again.

DATE COMPLETED: ....

It's often the small moments that can completely derail our days. There's a hole in our lives where interactions with our loved ones once lived.

You'll never replace those incredibly special moments, but it can be helpful to acknowledge them and the pain they cause. And perhaps begin to remember and integrate them in your present life, making them less painful as time goes on.

If you always called your loved one on the way home from work, can you now call a friend or family member and tell them how you're feeling? If every time you walk past their chair at the kitchen table you feel like you could burst into tears, can you leave a loving note there for yourself? If you always made pizza on Fridays, can you continue that tradition? If your loved one always walked through the door at 4 p.m., what can you do to make that time more comforting to you while keeping that memory alive?

Write about your thoughts on this difficult subject on the following page. What small, everyday moments come to mind? You're not going to replace them, but it can be helpful to write down what triggers you and then give your brain a new path, knowing with certainty that your memories are safe. Remember that it's perfectly normal to feel resistance, pain, and sadness. Just know that in time you'll start to feel more peace in these moments, especially if you acknowledge them.

Remember: this is a judgment-free zone. Write whatever comes to mind, without criticism.

We can often get stuck on a specific train of thought or a perpetual cascade of "what ifs." Can you relate? In therapy, my psychologist shared that when we don't have all the answers, our brains like to make up stories to fill in the blanks. And in those made-up stories, self-blame, guilt, and regrets can build.

I DIDN'T KNOW THAT SELF-BLAME WAS
A COMMON EXPERIENCE IN GRIEF...

. . .and I spent a long time being ashamed of the responsibility I felt for my dad's death. It doesn't matter that I wasn't actually responsible; for decades I lived with the feeling that I could have and should have done something more or that I shouldn't have said the things I did as a thirteen-year-old who didn't understand addiction like I do now.

What helped was turning to the facts and asking, "What do I know to be true?"

Have you ever heard the saying, "Don't believe everything you think"? It's a powerful reminder to check in with yourself and ask if your brain is trying to fill in the blanks of unknown details, or if you're ruminating too heavily about what you can't change.

When you write down some of these fears or worries, you release the chokehold they have over you. And you don't even have to write them here. It's proven that writing what you're feeling, even if you burn the pages or rip them into shreds, still reduces your cognitive load.

The more fears and worries we keep inside, the more we trap and amplify them. There's an old myth that talking about things makes them feel more real. In reality, sharing them releases them. Try to remind yourself of this often.

WHEN YOU FIND YOURSELF IN
SPIRALING THOUGHTS
AND WHAT IFS,

ASK YOURSELF:

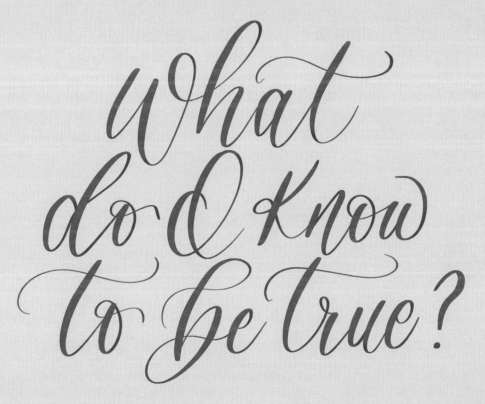

What
do I know
to be true?

START HERE WITH SOME OF THE MOST COMMON SPIRALING THOUGHTS

Self-compassion is a skill and a journey. If you're experiencing any feelings of guilt or self-blame, know that it's a common part of grieving and that help is available. It doesn't make you love them less to love yourself. See the Resources section (page 136) for helpful groups and guidance on asking for help.

Be open and honest in your answers below, releasing the grip they have over you. And the next time you find yourself in a spiral of "what ifs" or overwhelming thoughts, grab a blank piece of paper or open a notes app on your phone and freewrite. Then delete the note or tear it up.

I WISH WE COULD HAVE ONE LAST _____

_____

_____

_____

_____

_____

I WISH I WOULD HAVE SAID _____

_____

_____

_____

_____

_____

_____

I WISH I NEVER SAID _____

_____

_____

_____

_____

_____

_____

I CAN'T STOP THINKING ABOUT _____

_____

_____

_____

_____

_____

_____

I CAN BE KINDER TO MYSELF BY _____

_____

_____

_____

_____

_____

_____

_____

One of my most treasured possessions is a cross my dad carved out of wood and made into a necklace with a leather strap. Without fail over the last two decades, I've worn it to get through all my most difficult days. I put the strap over my neck, hold the cross tightly in one hand, and speak directly to him with tear-filled eyes.

WHETHER IT'S AN ITEM OF CLOTHING OR ONE OF THEIR POSSESSIONS PASSED DOWN TO YOU, WRITE ABOUT SOMETHING THAT BELONGED TO YOUR LOVED ONE AND HOW IT BRINGS YOU COMFORT: _____

_____

_____

_____

_____

A "sign" of ours is dimes. These coins seem to appear in the most unlikely places at the most needed times. Whenever one crosses mine, my mom's, or my sister's path, we take that as a message from my dad that he's with us.

WHAT ARE YOUR "SIGNS" FROM YOUR PERSON? WHAT WOULD YOU LIKE TO SEE MORE OF TO FEEL THAT THEY'RE WITH YOU? BE SPECIFIC: _____

_____

_____

_____

_____

_____

WRITE ABOUT ANY DREAMS THAT STAND OUT TO YOU SINCE
YOUR LOVED ONE DIED: _____

_____

_____

_____

_____

_____

_____

_____

_____

_____

_____

IF YOU HAVE SPIRITUAL OR RELIGIOUS BELIEFS ABOUT THE
AFTERLIFE, WRITE ABOUT THEM HERE. HAVE YOUR BELIEFS
CHANGED AT ALL SINCE YOUR LOVED ONE DIED? _____

_____

_____

_____

_____

_____

_____

_____

_____

Maybe you've already experienced this. The "Wow, they would have loved this" feeling as you stare out at a new incredible view, or you're surrounded by family in a place that your loved one adored.

What places or sights remind you of your loved one?

WHENEVER I'M HERE, I THINK OF YOU: _____

_____

_____

_____

_____

_____

IF YOU COULD HAVE GONE ANYWHERE, IT WOULD HAVE BEEN

_____

_____

_____

_____

_____

For my dad, it's the mountains. He was such an outdoors enthusiast. He loved skiing and would take my sister and I on "nature walks" every weekend we spent with him. Picnics in the park, stops at the local deli, and tent camping in the middle of nowhere are some of my fondest memories of growing up. Whenever I'm standing on the peak of a mountain and look down at the valley below, I'm filled with a knowing that my dad would love it there. It makes me feel closer to him.

there will
be Moments
when it hurts
to be happy.
Do it
anyway.

It's hard to see people traveling, falling in love, laughing, and seemingly moving on while your world feels like it's stopped turning. And in the early days of loss, that happiness might not ever feel possible for you, or it might feel ridden with guilt. It might feel bad to be happy, as contradictory—and yet valid—as that is.

But you will feel happiness again, in your own time. You'll never move on, but you'll move forward. And part of that experience is carrying your grief alongside your newfound joy. The melancholy will always be there alongside it, but it's joy and it's worth experiencing nonetheless. Look ahead to the Learn section (page 100) for a theory on growing around your grief.

THIS IS HOW WE EXPERIENCED JOY TOGETHER:

WHEN I THINK ABOUT US LAUGHING TOGETHER, THIS IS WHAT COMES TO MIND:

Your capacity to experience joy will change as time passes. Ask yourself this: Based on where I am in my grieving process, how can I try to find small joys every day? It could be a walk outside. Noticing the song of a bird. Laughing at your favorite show. Having coffee with a friend. Making your loved one's favorite recipe once it's not too painful to reenter the kitchen. Try to integrate some of the ways you experienced joy with your loved one into your new reality. And come back to this list on particularly heavy days.

As a "celebrate everything" kind of person, I love finding ways to make other people feel special, to mark an occasion, and to make traditions. It could be helpful for you to be intentional about finding small ways to celebrate too.

WHAT COULD HAPPINESS OR JOY LOOK LIKE FOR ME NOW?

the more
good things
you look for
the more
good things
you see...

ACCEPTING & GIVING LOVE

Having people to count on and be comforted by is an essential part of healing. Not everyone knows the right things to say or exactly how to help; some might even make your grief feel heavier. Reflect on your support system and how it's shaping your experience of grief. Your answers here will change with each passing month and year.

WHAT DOES LOVE LOOK LIKE FOR ME RIGHT NOW?

_____
_____
_____
_____
_____
_____
_____

WHAT DOES SUPPORT LOOK LIKE? DO I NEED SUPPORT IN WAYS I'M NOT CURRENTLY RECEIVING IT? _____

_____
_____
_____
_____
_____
_____
_____
_____

Talk about who you're grieving with and how that's shaping your own experience. Part of the complex journey of grieving is that you can also become a host to other people's grief. And sometimes it won't look like yours or it might feel even more overwhelming. There's no right way to grieve, yet resentment and misunderstandings can build by experiencing loss so differently from person to person. Everyone grieves at their own pace and for as long as it takes.

WHO AM I SUPPORTING IN THEIR GRIEF AND HOW?

grief

I'M ALLOWED TO FEEL TWO THINGS AT ONCE

Joy

Reflect

REFLECT

Honoring Our Memories

....

LEAVING A LEGACY

I was most excited about writing and creating space for this section—probably because being a keeper of memories becomes more precarious as your life exceeds that of your loved one. Two decades into my grieving, culling old photographs and recalling stories of days past feel like soul-filling activities. But it wasn't always that way.

It is such a relief to know that these pages will allow what feels like fragile fragments of my life with my dad to go into safekeeping. That's what I hope for you too.

Let's be
what we
most loved
about who
we lost

How did they love Me?

HOW CAN I REMEMBER THAT AND
HOW CAN I LOVE MYSELF MORE IN THEIR HONOR?

Recently, I read an essay I wrote about my dad three years after he passed away. More than a decade after writing it, I laughed out loud reading those words, and then proceeded to cry because those memories had faded almost entirely.

I don't think it's possible for us to forget the essence of our people or the way they made us feel. But it's truly another tragedy in itself that we can't just bottle up every word they ever said and every memory made.

Now that I have a daughter, it's imperative to me that I share her grandpa with her. For you, too, these pages will become source material for years to come.

What do you want to remember most? How did your loved one leave such a lasting impact? How can others in your circle help build a vivid picture of a life well-lived and loved?

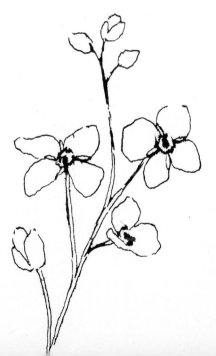

One day you'll be able to say their name without crying, and sharing a memory will be sad but will not leave you feeling broken. Below is a sample modern calligraphy script. Feel free to trace it or use your own handwriting to write your loved one's name on the following page.

Aa Bb Cc Dd

Ee Ff Gg Hh

Ii Jj Kk Ll

Mm Nn Oo Pp

Qq Rr Ss Tt

Uu Vv Ww

Xx Yy Zz

WHAT WAS YOUR LOVED ONE'S NAME? WRITE IT BELOW:

A VIVID PICTURE

What picture is vivid in your mind? Is it based on a photograph or a memory? What color is their hair? What are they wearing, down to the color of their sweater? Be as detailed as you can.

YOU ARE, WERE, AND WILL FOREVER BE MY (father, husband, grandparent, etc.) _____

_____

_____

_____

_____

WHEN I PICTURE YOU, I SEE _____

_____

_____

_____

_____

_____

_____

_____

_____

_____

_____

THE HARDEST PART IS

the Missing & the Wishing

Try not to censor yourself or come up with the perfect words here. Write what you would say if your loved one was sitting across from you. *What do I want you to know?*

THERE AREN'T ENOUGH WORDS TO CAPTURE WHAT YOU MEAN TO ME, BUT I'LL TRY. HERE'S WHAT YOU NEED TO KNOW ABOUT OUR RELATIONSHIP THAT'S AS TRUE NOW AS IT ALWAYS WILL BE: _____

_____

_____

_____

_____

_____

_____

_____

_____

_____

_____

_____

_____

_____

IF I HAD TO PICK THREE WORDS TO DESCRIBE YOU, I WOULD CHOOSE:

① _____

② _____

③ _____

WHEN I THINK ABOUT YOUR OUTLOOK ON LIFE OR WAY OF
LIVING, THIS IS WHAT COMES TO MIND: _____

_____

_____

_____

_____

_____

_____

_____

YOU WERE HAPPIEST WHEN _____

_____

_____

_____

_____

_____

_____

_____

SOMETIMES, YOU STRUGGLED WITH _____

_____

_____

_____

_____

_____

_____

YOU LOVED

_____
_____
_____
_____
_____
_____

YOUR GREATEST ACHIEVEMENTS OR PROUDEST MOMENTS
WERE

_____
_____
_____
_____
_____
_____

I KNOW YOU'D WANT TO BE REMEMBERED FOR

_____
_____
_____
_____
_____
_____

YOU SUPPORTED ME BY

_____
_____
_____
_____
_____

WITHOUT YOU, I NEVER COULD HAVE _____

_____

_____

_____

_____

_____

_____

EVERYONE ALWAYS SAID YOU WERE _____

_____

_____

_____

_____

_____

_____

_____

WHAT'S A UNIVERSAL TRUTH ABOUT YOUR LOVED ONE? WHAT
CHARACTERISTICS MADE THEM A GOOD FRIEND, PARENT, OR
PARTNER (ETC.)? _____

_____

_____

_____

_____

_____

_____

ADDING TO THE STORY

What are some stories others have shared with you about your loved one? Did anything surprise you? Seek out these stories as a way to connect with others who were close to your loved one.

ASK THREE PEOPLE WHO KNEW YOUR LOVED ONE WELL TO DESCRIBE THEM IN THREE WORDS. WHAT DID THEY SAY?

NAME:

① _____
② _____
③ _____

NAME:

① _____
② _____
③ _____

NAME:

① _____
② _____
③ _____

WHAT DO I WANT TO KNOW MORE ABOUT? WHO CAN I ASK?

At my father's funeral, and in the decades afterward, I adored hearing stories people told me about him as a child or a memory they shared together. My aunt remains the greatest source of all things pre-fatherhood about my dad. Is there someone who comes to mind for you? It's telling stories and finding laughter that can help us heal amidst the missing and the wishing they were here.

TRADITIONS

THESE WERE SOME OF OUR TRADITIONS THAT I WANT TO
REMEMBER AND POTENTIALLY CONTINUE: _____

_____

_____

_____

_____

_____

_____

_____

_____

_____

_____

_____

_____

_____

_____

_____

_____

_____

_____

_____

_____

_____

_____

_____

For me, it was repeating "1, 2, 3, 4" before hanging up every phone call with my dad, playing hairdresser as a child, him making up stories before bed, and going on nature walks.

Reminder: use the Letters to You section to expand on any memories or thoughts on which you want to go deeper.

OUR FIRST MEMORY TOGETHER (Be as descriptive as possible. Where were you? What was the weather? What did the room look like?):

OUR LAST MEMORY THAT I WANT TO REMEMBER (Try not to focus on the moment of their death here, as painful as that moment may be. Use your words to describe one of your last memories that you do want to remember. If you're ready to talk about their death, use the Letters to You section at the back of this journal to write to your loved one describing that day and the lasting impact it's had on you.): _____

_____

_____

_____

_____

_____

_____

_____

_____

_____

_____

_____

_____

_____

_____

_____

_____

_____

_____

_____

_____

_____

_____

_____

_____

A FEW MEMORIES THAT STAND OUT ABOVE ALL ELSE AND WHY

(Think about the way your loved one greeted you. The way they said goodbye on the phone or at the door or right before you both went to bed. Think about your history together and the little things you want to be sure are here on these pages for decades to come.): _____

MUSIC

Hearing specific songs can at once feel comforting, triggering, soul-filling, or gut-wrenching. But music is also a powerful tool for reducing stress, anxiety, and depression.

Music is also one of the greatest conjurers of memories. Pay attention to how songs that remind you of your loved one will start playing on the radio while you're driving or while you're walking through the mall. It's perhaps in these small moments that your person is making their love known to you.

Sometimes, hearing a song may derail your day. Other times, it will lift you up or fill you to the brim with nostalgia. Read the Cope section (page 38) again for tips on dealing with particularly difficult moments or days.

Since my dad passed about two decades ago, many of the songs on my list are ones that he would have never heard. It's simply the lyrics that spoke so well to my experience at that moment or a general feeling about our relationship.

SONGS THAT MAKE ME THINK OF YOU:

SONGS THAT MAKE ME CRY:

SONGS THAT LIFT ME UP: _____

_____

_____

_____

_____

_____

_____

SONGS THAT WERE YOUR FAVORITE: _____

_____

_____

_____

_____

_____

_____

MORE SONGS THAT REMIND ME OF YOU: _____

_____

_____

_____

_____

_____

_____

PROJECT IDEA: Come back to this page as you think of more songs, and then create a playlist of all the ones you write down. Listen to this playlist on particularly hard days (see page 44) as a way to lean into how you're feeling.

FREEWRITE: Use the Letters to You section at the back of this journal to freewrite about a song that stands out to you most and why.

HONORING YOU

How can you continue to honor your loved one? Use these prompts as a
starting point.

I'LL HONOR YOU BY DOING _____

_____

_____

_____

_____

_____

I'LL HONOR YOU BY SAYING _____

_____

_____

_____

_____

_____

I'LL HONOR YOU BY FEELING _____

_____

_____

_____

_____

_____

_____

I'LL HONOR YOU BY SHARING _____

_____

_____

_____

_____

_____

_____

_____

_____

_____

I'LL HONOR YOU BY BEING _____

_____

_____

_____

_____

_____

_____

_____

_____

_____

_____

_____

_____

FREEWRITE: Use the Letters to You section at the back of this journal to free-write about one of the statements you just wrote.

PHOTOGRAPHS

It's not often we print photographs anymore. I use the same five photos of my dad to show my daughter who her grandpa is. Even as a baby, she'd reach out and kiss his picture—indistinguishable from the moving FaceTime images of her family living across the country. To her, that's her grandpa and always will be, even though they'll never meet in life.

When my dad died, most of our photo albums went into storage bins, and I'd capture the odd picture with my phone to save in an album when I felt ready or it was necessary in moments of sadness to see my dad.

Some days you need to put the photos away and focus on the present. On others, memory-seeking and memory-keeping are exactly the comfort you need.

When you're ready, take time to find or print out ten of your favorite photos. Like this entire process, collecting photos isn't meant to be rushed. Take time to add them slowly, and they'll be here in this book forever. Maybe they reflect the memories you shared on the previous pages, or maybe they show the other ways you honored or continue to honor your relationship.

You'll be glad to have them here, in a single place, that you can always come back to and share with your loved ones.

INSERT PHOTO HERE

DATE: ....

WHY I INCLUDED THIS PHOTO: _____

_____

_____

_____

_____

_____

_____

_____

INSERT PHOTO HERE

DATE: ....

WHY I INCLUDED THIS PHOTO: _____

_____

_____

_____

_____

_____

_____

_____

INSERT PHOTO HERE

DATE: ....

WHY I INCLUDED THIS PHOTO: _____

INSERT PHOTO HERE

DATE: ....

WHY I INCLUDED THIS PHOTO: _____

_____

_____

_____

_____

_____

_____

_____

_____

INSERT PHOTO HERE

DATE: ....

WHY I INCLUDED THIS PHOTO: _____

INSERT PHOTO HERE

DATE: ....

WHY I INCLUDED THIS PHOTO: _____

_____

_____

_____

_____

_____

_____

_____

INSERT PHOTO HERE

DATE: ....

WHY I INCLUDED THIS PHOTO: _____

_____

_____

_____

_____

_____

_____

_____

INSERT PHOTO HERE

DATE: ....

WHY I INCLUDED THIS PHOTO: _____

_____

_____

_____

_____

_____

_____

_____

INSERT PHOTO HERE

DATE:

WHY I INCLUDED THIS PHOTO:

INSERT PHOTO HERE

DATE : ....

WHY I INCLUDED THIS PHOTO : _____

_____

_____

_____

_____

_____

_____

_____

INSERT PHOTO HERE

DATE: ....

WHY I INCLUDED THIS PHOTO: _____

_____

_____

_____

_____

_____

_____

_____

PROJECT IDEA: Scan your loved one's handwriting from a card they wrote in, find a loving line from an email, or save a screenshot of a meaningful text message they sent you. Get it printed on archival-quality paper and find a frame with a matte to display it in your home. You could also find a frame with two slots and include an image of them next to their message.

The first piece of artwork I hung in our daughter's nursery was from a card my dad wrote. I scanned his handwriting and got it printed on beautiful paper to be framed and matted, honored, and adored.

I never thought this simple piece would be so special to me, but handwriting is inherently special. It's personal. It carries the writer's emotions and personality, their actual hand. If you have any cards or letters from your loved ones, save them here.

And perhaps you'll be inspired to create a piece of art for your own home as well.

I think
I'll miss
you for
the rest
of my life

AND THAT'S OKAY

Learn

LEARN

Who Am I Now?

....

I wrote in the Introduction that "however you're experiencing grief right now, it won't be the place you stay." And I think this statement rings true about ourselves too. Death changes your reality, and with it your identity.

You could be grieving your old life right alongside the person you're missing. Grieving what could have been, or who you would have been if they hadn't died.

You could be scared of the unknown, unwilling or unsure of how to take the next step forward without them. Or you could be wishing the days away in search of a more peaceful future. These thoughts are normal and part of what makes grieving so complicated.

But here's one fact: we're only guaranteed the present.

THE HERE AND NOW.

YOU KNOW THIS MORE THAN EVER.

Whether you're here and filled with despair, or you're starting to see small slivers of hope in between, your grief will always be a part of you. Your life will just slowly begin to grow bigger around it. Be in pursuit of the growing.

Moving
forward
not moving
on

The age-old saying "time heals all wounds" isn't exactly true. In Dr. Lois Tonkin's theory, grief represents a dark circle that takes over your entire life when someone you love dies. Instead of that dark circle getting smaller over time, she states that your life will start to grow around and with it. The grief stays the same size, but you start to build more experiences, more moments of joy, and more life around the sorrow.

Sometimes, in the middle of that living, grief interrupts, and the cycle continues. The more you live, the more that initial grief circle isn't the largest part of your life, but it's still at its core. You live with and grow around your grief.

In the Introduction, I talked about my dad's death being the centerpiece of my life. His death doesn't feel like a "before & after" but, rather, like life revolves around it. If you visualize this as a table, my dad's death and my grief are the centerpiece and the new moments of my life—joy-filled experiences (graduating from school, getting married, having a baby, celebrating birthdays and anniversaries) and other losses—simply join the tablescape. They elevate and change it; they elevate and change me.

LOVING MYSELF AS YOU LOVED ME

Consider this question: "How can I treat myself more like how my person loved me?"

This is completely different from "What would they want me to do?" Instead, it's about asking yourself who you were to the person you lost and how to live more into that. How to love yourself alongside the missing and the longing. How to be inspired by their love for you and guided by it.

Before writing, I recommend reading the poem called "On Those Days" written by Donna Ashworth that inspired this reflection.

WHO WAS I TO MY LOVED ONE? HOW DID THEY LOVE ME?

WHAT ARE THREE WORDS THEY WOULD HAVE USED TO DESCRIBE ME?

①
②
③

HOW CAN I LIVE MORE LIKE HOW THEY LOVED ME? _____

By having the courage to endure your grief, by learning how to survive what you never thought you could, your sense of self and what's important is expanding.

You're changing. You wish it never happened, but you're growing. And all the while, your love for the person you lost remains the same. Take solace in that.

Talking about living doesn't bring upon death, just like saying you're in pain doesn't suddenly make life worse. It's okay to both want a future and be resistant to it. Just know that your love for your loved one never fades, even as you receive more.

Return to these questions often over the coming months and years so that you can recognize any patterns or changes.

HOW HAS MY PERCEPTION OF LIFE AND DEATH CHANGED?

YOUR DEATH HAS TAUGHT ME _____

_____

_____

_____

_____

_____

_____

_____

HOW HAVE MY PRIORITIES SHIFTED? _____

_____

_____

_____

_____

_____

_____

_____

_____

I HAVE MORE CLARITY ABOUT _____

_____

_____

_____

_____

_____

_____

_____

WHAT ADVICE WOULD I GIVE TO A FRIEND GOING THROUGH A
SIMILAR LOSS?

I KNOW YOU WOULD WANT ME TO

I KNOW I NEED TO

I'M LEARNING _____

_____

_____

_____

_____

_____

_____

YOU WOULD BE SO PROUD BECAUSE _____

_____

_____

_____

_____

_____

_____

_____

I'M PROUD OF MYSELF FOR _____

_____

_____

_____

_____

_____

_____

_____

_____

You Can't Feel too Much or for too Long

NAME AT LEAST THREE THINGS YOU'RE GRATEFUL FOR

When you're naming what you're grateful for, try to be specific beyond big categories like home or health. Whether it's the way your dog greets you in the morning, or how the sun shines through the living room windows at 3 p.m. What brings you small bouts of joy and why? Consider coming back to this page and making this a daily practice.

ONE

TWO

THREE

STAYING GROUNDED

Being present doesn't erase the past or make your pain disappear—it simply helps you stay grounded and build new experiences without being all-consumed by grief. Whenever you revisit the past, whether through writing in this journal or reminiscing over photographs and videos, it's important to ground yourself back in the present again. Revisit the mindfulness techniques in the Rest section (page 20) for breathing and art exercises and check the Resources section (page 136) for more ideas to get inspired.

WHAT HELPS ME STAY PRESENT? WHAT MEDITATION OR MINDFULNESS ART PRACTICES RESONATE WITH ME OR AM I INTERESTED IN TRYING?

SCARED OF
THE FUTURE

HOPEFUL FOR
MORE PEACE

EXCITED ABOUT
SOMETHING

IT'S OKAY TO BE FEELING
EVERY EMOTION RIGHT NOW

GUILTY FOR
FEELING HAPPY

LONGING FOR
YOUR
OLD LIFE

OVERWHELMED BY
FEELING IT
ALL AT ONCE

THE POWER OF AFFIRMATIONS

Words matter, and how we talk to ourselves does too. This exercise might feel uncomfortable, or even cheesy—that's normal! But if there's one thing I've learned about grieving, it's not to believe everything you think. Where our beliefs around grief and loss are often rooted in fear and not love, affirmations give us a much-needed dose of acceptance, hope, and safety.

Think of these as mindset swaps. Changing your perspective on grieving is not about becoming more positive; it's about remaining or becoming empowered.

WHAT ARE SOME THINGS YOU MIGHT HATE TO ADMIT YOU BELIEVE? HOW CAN YOU SHIFT YOUR MINDSET TO BE MORE SELF-COMPASSIONATE?

BELIEF		AFFIRMATION
WHEN YOU THINK: *I shouldn't be this sad.*	→	REMIND YOURSELF: *It's normal to be this sad and I'm allowed to feel this way.*
WHEN YOU THINK: *I should have moved on by now.*	→	REMIND YOURSELF: *I'll never move on, but I will move forward; I'm taking small steps every day.*
WHEN YOU THINK: *I can't be happy without them.*	→	REMIND YOURSELF: *Being happy doesn't take away my love. My happiness will grow around my grief.*

BELIEF		AFFIRMATION
WHEN YOU THINK: *I can't do anything but grieve.*	→	REMIND YOURSELF: *This is the hardest thing I've ever gone through, and I'm giving it my all, but it won't always feel this heavy.*
WHEN YOU THINK: *I'll never be the same person again.*	→	REMIND YOURSELF: *And that's okay.*
WHEN YOU THINK: *No one knows what to say or how to help me.*	→	REMIND YOURSELF: *I don't need to accept extended hands every time they're offered, but I will ask for what I need.*
WHEN YOU THINK: *I can't stop thinking about how they died.*	→	REMIND YOURSELF: *If it stops me from having hope or living fully, I'll get help to overcome this.*
WHEN YOU THINK: *I'm going to forget all our memories.*	→	REMIND YOURSELF: *I could never forget you, and now I know that our memories are here, in this book, and in my mind forever.*
	→	
	→	
	→	

Read the list of affirmations below and pick three statements to put somewhere you'll see them every day. Add your own words of encouragement in the blank squares when inspirations comes.

I CAN DO HARD THINGS.

I'M IN CONTROL OF MY MIND.

NO MATTER WHAT HAPPENS TODAY, I CAN GET THROUGH IT.

I'M MOVING FORWARD, NOT MOVING ON.

I'M PATIENT

WITH MY HEALING.

I AM GENTLE

WITH MYSELF.

I'LL LOVE MYSELF

AS THEY LOVED ME.

I AM SAFE.

PARTING WORDS

Thank you for choosing to share your heart here.

You're brave and you're strong, even though you didn't choose to be. You're capable of living a wonderful life and loving yourself enough to make that happen—both for yourself and in honor of your loved one.

Throughout this journal, I hope you felt safe. Relieved. Empowered. Understood. And overall, I hope you feel some semblance of hope for living with and growing around your grief.

Because even though grief is forever, so too is love. And you're brimming with it.

You're on my heart and in my prayers, friend. And remember:

YOU'RE CREATIVE

Write or do something creative every day and see how it improves your mood. Create to slow down. To reduce stress. To tap back into the present after revisiting the past. Create to express, not to impress.

YOU'RE HOPEFUL

An easy way to continue journaling is to freewrite in response to the following prompts at the beginning or end of every single day:

- What are three things you're grateful for?
- What are three things you want to let go of? (These can be fears, a particular mindset, or actual things.)
- What gives you hope?

Be gentle on yourself

Within your words is your healing

YOU'RE CHANGING

Keep coming back to this journal one month, six months, and years from now to see how much your answers change. I promise they will.

YOU'RE ASKING FOR & GIVING HELP

If your struggle feels too intense or traumatic today or at any point in the future, consider asking for help from your community, loved ones, therapy, or otherwise. You'll be stronger for it. And remember that helping others can also help your own well-being when you have time or energy to give.

YOU'RE NOT ALONE

I'm the artist behind Peak Paper Co. and created all the artwork within this journal. Find digital downloads of the quotes here, along with more journaling prompts, art classes, and grief resources on my website at www.peakpaperco.com/journal.

Let's be friends! I would be honored if you'd say hello and share your journey with me on Instagram: @peakpaperco.

LETTERS TO YOU

Use these pages immediately upon receiving this journal or whenever the feeling strikes. Write to your loved one about your intention behind putting pen to paper. Expand on some of the creative prompts you've answered. Tell them about a particularly hard or surprisingly good day when they made their love known to you. Release any thoughts you're spiraling or ruminating on. And remember: write to express, not to impress.

DATE:

DEAR _____ ,

DATE:

DEAR _____,

DATE: ....

DEAR _____ ,

DATE: ....

DEAR _____ ,

DATE: ....

DEAR _____,

DATE: ....

DEAR _____ ,

DATE:

DEAR _____,

DATE:

DEAR _____,

DATE:

DEAR _____ ,

DATE:

DEAR _____,

DATE: ....

DEAR _____,

RESOURCES

Lots of self-discovery and research went into the making of this journal. Following are suggested books, podcasts, apps, and other tools I have personally leaned on and encourage you to explore too. I'd also love for you to share this list with your friends and family.

 Scan the QR code for links to all the books, podcasts, and apps I've recommended here.

GRIEF SUPPORT

LOSS: POEMS TO BETTER WEATHER THE MANY WAVES OF GRIEF BY DONNA ASHWORTH

This book of poetry feels like a warm hug. A wonderful gift for fellow grievers and a reminder for all of us that we're not as alone as we often feel.

HEALING WITH DAVID KESSLER (PODCAST, GRIEF.COM) AND TENDER HEARTS GRIEF GROUP

David Kessler is a prominent grief expert who contributed to The Five Stages of Grief, a theory that has now evolved to reflect the complex range of human experience. He believes in the power of writing to heal and that "what we resist pursues us, what we face transforms us." On his podcast, he interviews internationally recognized grievers and explores complex topics with other experts on guilt, self-blame, trauma, and finding meaning through our grief.

UNTANGLE GRIEF (WEBSITE & APP)

This app and its social media pages are an online peer support group to help people ask questions and navigate life after death together. I love their

Instagram page where they share "untold stories" of grief from members and relatable words from people all over the world. The comments are full of insightful reflections and deep longing.

GRIEF WORKS (BOOK & APP)

Grief Works is an incredibly moving book written by leading psychotherapist Julia Samuel. She's a firm believer that we need to allow grief to storm through us, get chaotic and messy, and ultimately change us. She introduced me to the concept of post-traumatic growth and kairos vs. chronos time, referenced in this journal. The Grief Works grief support app is something I recommend everyone download who is in the early days of grief—it's well worth the investment to glean her guidance. It functions like a guided digital journal, with helpful videos and prompts along the way.

THE HAPPINESS LAB (PODCAST) BY DR. LAURIE SANTOS

Dr. Laurie Santos researches the science of happiness and shares how to find more of it by understanding our painful emotions and experiences. It's empowering to learn how our brains are wired and how we can change that wiring!

DARING GREATLY AND ATLAS OF THE HEART BY DR. BRENÉ BROWN

Dr. Brené Brown is an expert on vulnerability and shares how it has the power to change the way we grieve, lead, love, work, parent, and educate for the better. Her work has transformed the way I function decades into my grieving process, and I probably quote something she's written at least once a day in casual conversation.

THERAPY OR CRISIS HELPLINES:

In the United States: To reach a trained crisis counselor for free, 24 hours a day, seven days a week, call or text 988. You can also go to 988lifeline.org or dial the current toll-free number 800-273-8255 [TALK].

In Canada: If you or someone you know is in immediate crisis, please call 1-833-456-4566 toll-free (in QC: 1-866-277-3553) 24/7 or visit talksuicide.ca. Text to 45645 (4 p.m. – midnight ET). You can also visit wellnesstogether.ca for more resources and to connect one-on-one with a counselor.

BetterHelp.com is an online counseling service currently available in the United States and Canada.

MEDITATION & MINDFULNESS

ON PURPOSE (PODCAST) BY JAY SHETTY

After living as a monk and now running the number one health and wellness podcast (2022), Jay Shetty shares wisdom and teachings on living life intentionally, with integrity, and in the present. His teachings are beginner-friendly and culturally relevant—they're what introduced me to mindfulness and meditation.

TEN PERCENT HAPPIER (PODCAST, BOOK & APP) BY DAN HARRIS

Dan Harris shares how to meditate and the research behind it, and interviews leading experts in the field to understand some of the most complex human experiences.

CALM (APP)

I have a yearly subscription to Calm and love the daily meditations. There are also meditations to help you fall asleep, grieve, and learn how to settle your mind. Try to do five-minute meditations (or more) daily to see a huge impact on your ability to regulate your emotions.

ZENTANGLE ART

Even if you say you "don't have an artistic bone in your body," doodling is easy and can help you tap into a flow state. Search for zentangle designs online and recreate your own using strokes with simple pen and ink. Also, try continuous line drawings.

CALLIGRAPHY & WATERCOLOR CLASSES WITH BRITTANY (PEAKPAPERCO.COM)

Art is good for you. Writing, painting, and calligraphy are all proven practices to help alleviate anxiety, decrease stress, and improve your overall well-being. I teach beginners how to get creative again with art kits, virtual classes, and workshops across North America.

BRITTANY'S BOOK RECOMMENDATIONS FOR CREATIVE LIVING

THE ARTIST'S WAY BY JULIA CAMERON
BIG MAGIC BY ELIZABETH GILBERT
THE CREATIVE ACT BY RICK RUBIN

Each of these books reminds you how to reignite your sense of awe and wonder, and how we're all creative beings. I'll read these cover to cover hundreds of times over the course of my life and hope they inspire a new journey back to creativity for you too. Remember: we're all creative. Yes, you too!

YOUR BRAIN ON ART BY SUSAN MAGSAMEN AND IVY ROSS

Finally, a book filled with science-backed evidence supporting how essential creativity and the arts are to our well-being and mental health. A must-read! The evidence shows that pursuing and experiencing art can actually be given as prescriptions for trauma, grief, and PTSD, and that it adds years to our lives.

MUSIC TO MOVE YOU, "FORGET YOU NOT" PLAYLIST

Visit the QR code for a curated selection of songs from fellow grievers that remind us what it means to lose someone you love and still find comfort.

ACKNOWLEDGMENTS

GOD GRANT ME THE SERENITY TO ACCEPT THE
THINGS I CANNOT CHANGE,
THE COURAGE TO CHANGE THE THINGS I CAN,
AND THE WISDOM TO KNOW THE DIFFERENCE.

REINHOLD NIEBUHR, "THE SERENITY PRAYER"

To my late father, forever my "Daddy," Darryl Dakins. I know deep within my soul that you would be so proud of me. Not only for publishing this journal but for living a beautiful life. For walking a different path. One brimming with love and trust and creativity. One guided so deeply by our thirteen years together and now by the ever-present ache and lessons of your loss. I've felt you with me with every word I've written; every journal entry, essay, and photograph I unearthed in this process; every heart-to-heart with Mom and Katrina; every tear that I'll continue to shed; every time I hold your necklace close to my heart. I've loved you all my life and I always will.

To my mom, I am endlessly, eternally grateful for you. You're exactly what I aspire to be as a parent, and I only become more in awe of the nine lives you've already lived as I grow. Thank you for always believing my fears while championing my passions. For being two parents in one. For making good choices and showing us how. For selflessly carrying an impossible load so that we could have a relationship with our father. You are love personified and I'm incredibly blessed to be your daughter. I can't wait to write our next book together!

To my sister, my number one champion. My very best friend. Elizabeth Gilbert once said that there are people who dance and those who support the dancers—equally important roles. You are both. You've led the way our entire lives, showing me what empathy, sisterhood, motherhood, and unconditional love are. I know which steps to take and how to forge my own path because of you going first. I love you beyond measure.

To Grandma and Grandpa, thank you for showing me creativity. I would spend hours in your craft room surrounded by paint and glitter and pom-poms galore, and hours still writing poetry and painting pictures you'd frame around the house. You bought me my first easels and art supplies. You kept everything I ever wrote and still do. You taught me how to show love and how special it is to feel understood and believed in. What a gift!

To Bryan, Kevin, Kathleen, Frank, Brit, and Jon. My beloved nieces Olivia, Evi, and Veronica. Aunty Carolyn and Aunty Maureen. Our family means the world to me, and you're the very best.

To "the gurks," Molly, Julia, Cait, and Kim. Michelle, Jenny, Tara, and all my incredible friends who share my zest for celebrating the big and small ways that life can be so giving and heartbreaking all at once. Your words of wisdom and encouragement have meant everything in this process.

To my therapist. You taught me self-compassion and how grief can begin long before our loved ones die. You taught me how to release and accept the guilt, the anger, and the shame around losing a parent to addiction, all while still loving him so deeply. You showed me how to hold two truths at once. Without our sessions, I don't know that I could have felt so empowered to share these words.

To my teachers, thank you. I'm endlessly grateful that you started my journaling practice all those years ago and said I should "do something with this!" as a writer and as an artist. I have and will continue to.

To my editorial team at Paige Tate & Co., thank you for trusting my voice and my writing so unequivocally. Thank you for answering that first email and for all the happy tears I've cried from feeling so supported in making this dream a reality.

To all of my clients and friends who have supported and helped grow my art business to what it is today. Peak Paper Co. is a dream come true because of you!

To my loving husband, Scott, without whom this wildly beautiful life would not be possible. From traveling the world and moving across the country to starting our "little life" that's now a big one, your steadiness and perspective have always been my guide. There's no greater solace than hearing, "No matter what happens, I'll always love you." It's easy to take risks when you are my home.

And finally, to our daughter, Francesca. My Frankie Jean. My sweet girl. Your life was the catalyst for creating this journal and for everything good and great I'll ever do. Being your mom is soul-defining and it's a beautiful relief that you may come to know your grandpa through the words on these pages. May I continue to pass on what a gift it is to know you're truly cherished and capable of anything.

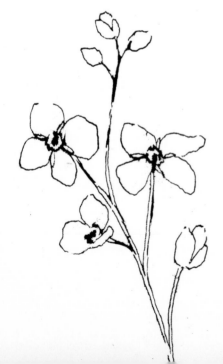

ABOUT THE AUTHOR

Brittany DeSantis is the artist behind Peak Paper Co., an heirloom art brand based in Alberta, Canada. Through her worldwide art partnerships and workshops across North America, she teaches beginners the power of getting creative again through writing, watercolor painting, and calligraphy lessons; live art events; and custom commissions. When Brittany lost her father at the age of thirteen, she turned to journaling as a way to cope. Decades later, writing continues to be her first love and a mainstay in her grief journey. She's on a mission to help others tap back into their creativity, commemorate their loved ones, and learn art as a means to heal.

Brittany lives in Edmonton with her husband, Scott; dog, Bubba; and beautiful daughter, Francesca. Living near the Canadian Rockies inspired her business name and continued awe for the outdoors. Alongside her passion for the arts, she adores her family, friends, food (eating it, not making it!), laughter, a full dining table, and heartfelt conversations that last into the wee hours of the morning. She believes that creativity, thoughtfulness, and gratitude are essential, that nature, dogs, and family are life's purest joys, and that art is always a gift worth giving.

Paige Tate & Co.

Published by Paige Tate & Co.

Paige Tate & Co. is an imprint of Blue Star Press

PO Box 8835, Bend, OR 97708

contact@bluestarpress.com

www.bluestarpress.com

Design by Megan Kesting

Photography by Tracey Jazmin and Dallas Curow

Artwork by Brittany DeSantis

ISBN: 9781958803370

Printed in China

10 9 8 7 6 5 4 3 2 1